ÉANNA NÍ LAMHNA

WONDERS OF THE WILD

ILLUSTRATED BY
BRIAN FITZGERALD

THE O'BRIEN PRESS
DUBLIN

CONTENTS

NATURE WILL SURPRISE YOU

When I was young there were no televisions or games consoles in Ireland — so hard to imagine now! After we came home from school we were sent outside to play. I lived in the countryside in County Louth, and playing outside meant climbing trees, looking for birds' nests — very carefully so as not to scare the birds, walking across the fields to a nearby pond, and other wildlife adventures.

I loved reading too, but it wasn't easy to find explanations for many of the things I noticed in the wild. And it still isn't today, even with all the information to be found online as well as in books.

Frogs hibernated at the bottom of the pond for months. How come they didn't drown? And what caused that sparkle on the sea at night that we noticed on our holidays?

Quite often the children's books just got it wrong too. The pictures of spiders, such as Little Miss Moffat, always had their legs in the wrong place! I knew that you could see squirrels — red ones — at any time of the year. Why did storybooks show them hibernating in winter?

I have always loved the unusual and the surprising. So, when I got the chance to write a book about wildlife for children, I knew I wanted to write about our weird and wonderful wildlife. The facts about rabbits and their poo and bats and their eyesight may surprise you. Even plants are sometimes not what they seem!

My hope is that this book will send you on a wonderful wildlife adventure and that you will start to notice even more amazing things when you are out and about in nature.

The artist for the book, Brian Fitzgerald, did lots of sketches using photographs to help him. With our designer, Emma Byrne, we put words and pictures on the pages, bringing the wonders of the wild to life for young readers — and their families and schools.

As our world faces many challenges, the more we all know about the natural world around us, and the more we care, the better.

Éanna Ní Lamhna

SPIDERS ARE CANNIBALS

Spiders do not have wings, but the
insects they eat do. To catch these,
some spiders spin a sticky web of threads,
called silk. They make this
silk in their abdomen and squirt the threads
out through special spinners from their
bottom end to make a web. Then the
spider waits nearby for dinner to arrive.

When a fly crashes into the web,
it gets stuck in the sticky threads.
The spider rushes across and kills the fly.
How come the spider doesn't get stuck in
its own sticky web? Believe it or not, it has
a non-stick coating on its legs
that means it doesn't stick to the web.

EYES

Most spiders have eight eyes, arranged in two rows
on the top of their head.

Cellar spiders have their eyes on short stalks.

CANNIBALS

As carnivores, spiders kill and eat insects, but they are also cannibals
and will kill and eat other spiders – even those of their own species.
There is only ever one spider per web.

Mating with a female spider can be very dangerous for the male. The male will
often bring a gift to the female when he visits. A tasty fly wrapped up in lots of silk
thread does the job nicely. The gift distracts the female and usually allows the male
to escape after mating.

LEGS

Spiders' bodies have two parts: their head and the lower part, called their abdomen.
They have eight legs, which are all attached to their head – four on each side!
There are no legs on the abdomen.

FANGS

Under their eyes, spiders have two fangs. These are very sharp, folded hollow teeth.
When a spider finds a victim, it quickly unfolds its fangs, stabs its prey and injects a
deadly venom from glands under its fangs. Spiders very rarely bite people. Mostly
their fangs cannot pierce our strong skin. The exception is the False Widow spider
which can if it feels trapped by us, but its bites are not fatal to humans.

EATING THEIR OWN POO

Nine hundred years ago rabbits were brought to Ireland by the Normans for food. As time went on, people did not want so many rabbits in their fields, so a disease of other wild animals, called myxomatosis, was deliberately spread into rabbits. This kills many rabbits every year. However, some rabbits are immune, and there are always plenty of rabbits around.

BREEDING
Rabbits breed very quickly. A female rabbit can live for four or five years in the wild and can give birth to 120 young.

AN EXTRA SPECIAL EYELID
Rabbits can sleep with their eyes open as they have a special third eyelid as well as their upper and lower eyelids. This is a clear membrane that they can see through and which they blink to keep their eye from drying out.

NO WASTE

Wild rabbits eat grass, which is very difficult to digest. It passes quickly through their stomach and intestines and there is still nourishment left in it by the time it reaches the end of their intestines. When this happens at night and the rabbit needs to do a poo, it eats it!

Then their waste goes through the digestive system for a second time, and this time round all the nourishment gets absorbed. When morning comes, the rabbit comes out of its burrow and does lots of small dry droppings on the grass nearby.

Black shiny poos are the ones rabbits eat. The dried-up balls that have been through the rabbit's system twice are the ones we see outside their burrows.

EATING UNTIL THEY BURST

Caterpillars eat until they burst – not just once but four times. Female butterflies lay their eggs on the food plant that the caterpillar needs to eat and then die. The eggs hatch out into tiny caterpillars that begin eating the leaves of the plant. They are eating machines. All day, they eat, digest the food, produce droppings – lots of those – and grow larger. Caterpillars have all their soft bits on the inside and their skin, their hard part, on the outside.

INSTAR

As they grow bigger and fatter, this skin does not stretch, so they burst! Their skin splits down the back, and a bigger, fatter caterpillar wriggles out to continue eating. Its new skin may be a different colour and may be hairier than the previous skin. Soon, the caterpillar is too big for this second skin, so it bursts again and has another new skin. Each of these stages is called an instar. The caterpillar bursts four times, until it reaches a fifth and final instar stage.

LOOKING HAIRY OR FIERCE

By this stage, it is big and fat and would make a nice meal for a bird. To avoid this, the caterpillar has become very hairy, and most birds avoid hairy caterpillars as they irritate their mouths. Other fifth instar caterpillars, while not hairy, can look fierce — another great way to keep the birds away.

I'm going to burst!

Garden Tiger moth caterpillar

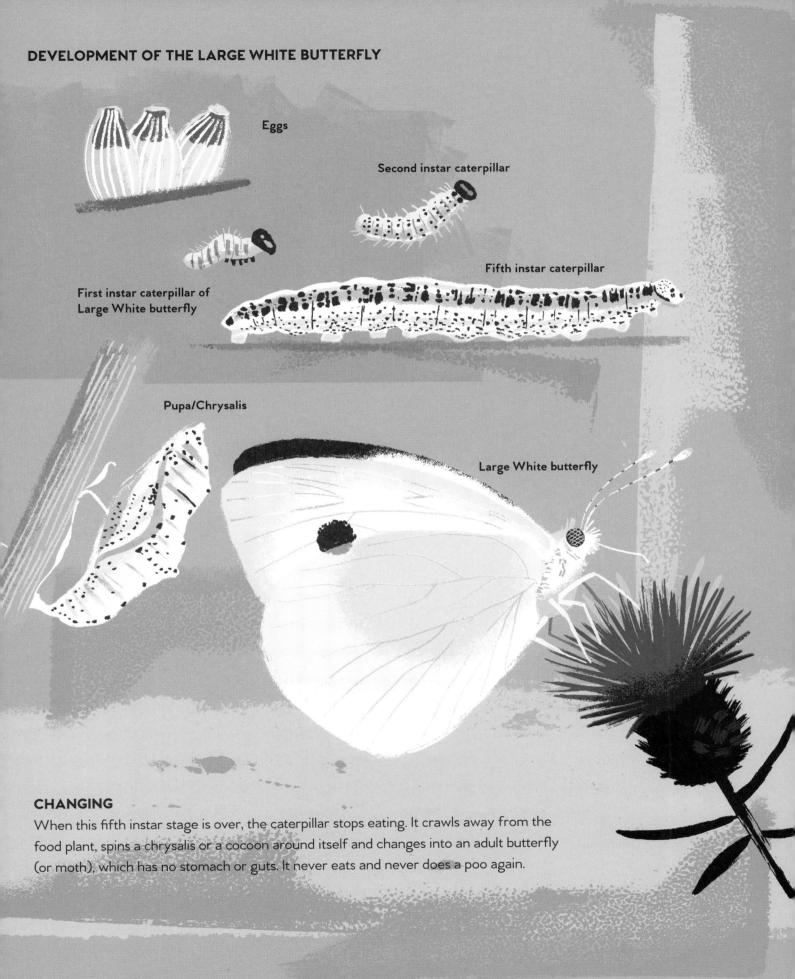

DEVELOPMENT OF THE LARGE WHITE BUTTERFLY

Eggs

Second instar caterpillar

First instar caterpillar of
Large White butterfly

Fifth instar caterpillar

Pupa/Chrysalis

Large White butterfly

CHANGING

When this fifth instar stage is over, the caterpillar stops eating. It crawls away from the
food plant, spins a chrysalis or a cocoon around itself and changes into an adult butterfly
(or moth), which has no stomach or guts. It never eats and never does a poo again.

11

FOREVER FLYING

Swifts are birds that fly very well but are not able to walk. They spend the first four years of their lives flying without stopping. The adults come to Ireland in May to breed and are gone by August – back up into the air for the next eight months.

HOW DO THEY EAT?

They get all their food from small insects that they catch while flying. They drink by grabbing sips of water as they fly over lakes and rivers.

HOW DO THEY SLEEP?

They sleep, up in the air. They soar on updraught winds, up to heights of 3,000 metres. Then they sleep while they glide – not for hours like humans, but enough to keep them going.

Swift

Swallow

House martin

Swifts

MATING AND LAYING EGGS

Swifts even mate up in the air. They only come down out of the skies to lay eggs and rear young. Their leg muscles are very weak as they never walk. If they landed on the ground, they would never take off again. So, they nest in holes in roofs, under broken roof slates, or in wall cavities. They use just a few feathers stuck together with saliva for their nest as it is difficult for them to gather material.

They lay two or three eggs and feed the young with small flies. When their chicks are big enough, they go to the edge of the nest and jump out into space. This is why the breeding site needs to be up high – swifts have to learn to fly very quickly!

Nesting swifts

THE IMPORTANCE OF COLOUR

Colour can mean the difference between life and death in the animal world. Carnivores are always looking for other animals to eat. One way of escaping from them is to look exactly like the background. In other words, to use camouflage.

Ladybird

GREEN AND RED

This is why creatures that feed on leaves are often green in colour. Caterpillars, greenflies and shield bugs are all green so that they are not easily spotted by hungry birds.

However, some insects are bright red in colour. How come they are not immediately gobbled up by hungry birds who see them on leaves?

Ladybirds have bright colours because they don't need to hide. They taste horrible and birds soon learn this if they ever eat one. Their colours act as a warning. Don't eat me!

Caterpillar of the Small White butterfly

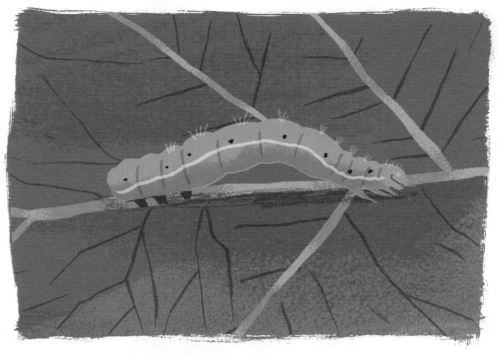

Caterpillar of the Cinnabar moth

Cinnabar moth

Ragwort

YOU WON'T LIKE ME!

Yellow and black are warning colours too. Birds in Ireland will not eat bees or wasps because they know that they could get stung in the mouth. Neither do they eat the black and yellow caterpillars of the Cinnabar moth because the colour warns them not to. These caterpillars taste terrible and contain poisons. They develop into moths that are red and black, more warning colours for birds to keep away.

PRETENDING TO BE SOMETHING ELSE

Getting eaten is always a danger to wildlife. Mimicry is another very good way to avoid this.

HOW TO FOOL THE BIRDS

Something that tastes delicious can look like something dangerous and fool predators into avoiding it. Bees and wasps are dangerous to birds. Other insects have the same black and yellow colours but have no sting and no bad taste.

Hoverflies look like wasps and fool the birds, but you will notice that they fly quite differently. Bee moths and Horntails are yellow and black too, and so they also escape being eaten.

Wasp

Horntail

Hoverfly

MASTERS OF MIMICRY

There are caterpillars that are so good at mimicry that they look exactly like a twig on a branch. This is what the caterpillar of the August Thorn does. The caterpillar of the Elephant Hawkmoth looks exactly like a small snake. Looking like a bird poo is excellent camouflage as well and this is what the Scalloped Hook-tip moth does.

August Thorn caterpillar, looking like a birch twig

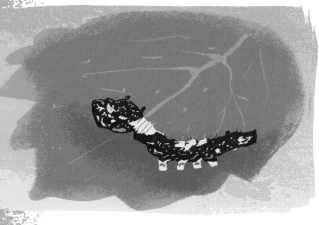

Scalloped Hook-tip caterpillar on birch, looking like a poo

Elephant Hawkmoth caterpillar, looking like a snake

BEE ORCHID

Flowers can be mimics as well. The flower of the Bee Orchid looks exactly like a species of solitary bee, so a male solitary bee looking for a female is fooled and tries to mate with it. It gets all covered with pollen as it does. When it then visits another orchid, the pollen it is carrying pollinates the second orchid, which was the orchid's plan all along. Eventually, the bee meets a real female bee and mates successfully.

BEES AS THE GOODY GOODIES

DIFFERENT TYPES OF BEES

The honeybee lives in a hive with a queen and up to 40, 000 female worker bees.

Bumblebees live in a nest built by the queen when she comes out of hibernation in spring. There are only about 400 female worker bees in these nests.

The third type of bee is called a solitary bee. These bees do not live in nests with a queen. Instead, each solitary bee builds an individual nest, in places such as banks or holes in the ground, and lays just a few eggs there.

All three types of bees collect pollen from flowers and bring it back to their young in special hairy pollen baskets on their back legs. This is made into pollen bread and fed to the growing bees. They never visit red garden flowers as bees cannot see the colour red.

Bumblebee with pollen baskets on legs

Honeybee

HONEY

Adult bees eat honey. To make this, the worker bees suck up nectar from the flowers and carry it back to the nest in their nectar sac. There are special worker bees there who turn the nectar into honey.

Honeybees make lots of honey because they eat it during the winter. Bumblebees only make enough for the summer as the workers all die when winter comes and the queen hibernates.

Adult solitary bees bring back pollen to feed their young, but they do not make honey. They just drink the nectar directly from the flower.

Orange-tailed Mining bee

WASPS ARE NOT BADDIES

Wasps are different from bees. They have shiny, not hairy, bodies, and they feed their young on chewed-up insects, such as greenflies, blackflies and whiteflies.

THE QUEEN AND WHAT WASPS EAT

All wasps die in the winter, except the queen. She hibernates and re-emerges in spring to build a nest and produce young.

She builds a small paper nest – the size of a golf ball – from chewed-up timber. She lays eight eggs in special cells. When they hatch out, she feeds them with chewed-up insects and they become the first worker wasps. These workers make the nest bigger and bigger. It can end up the size of a football. The queen lays lots more eggs in the cells and the worker wasps bring home insects to feed the young.

Adult wasps do not eat insects. They like sweet food. They get this in the nest from the baby wasps who vomit up a sugary liquid after they have been fed. The worker wasps lick this liquid off the baby wasps, and this is their food for the summer.

Wasps

WHEN AUTUMN AND WINTER COME

In August, the queen wasp dies of exhaustion, having laid 100 eggs each day since spring. The last eggs she lays become new queens and reproductive males called drones. They leave the nest to mate and the new queens hibernate until the next spring.

As there are no new baby wasps, there is no sugary food in the nest for the wasps. In September and October, those last wasps need to find sweet food elsewhere. They get it from fruit, or nectar, or the sweet food that people eat, such as jam, cakes or sugary drinks. This is why wasps annoy us in autumn.

When the weather turns colder, they all die. Their nest is never used again. The new queens always make a new nest in spring.

A wasps' nest.

WHY FROGS DON'T DROWN

Frogs are amphibians. This means that they are able to live on water and on land. When they are living on land, they breathe air into their lungs and so get the oxygen that they need.

HIBERNATION

Frogs hibernate for three or four months at the bottom of ponds. They cannot breathe air into their lungs then. If they tried, they would breathe in water and drown.

HOW DO FROGS SURVIVE UNDERWATER?

Fish, which live in water all the time, have gills to extract oxygen from the water, but frogs do not have any gills. They get oxygen directly from the water through their skin. This oxygen moves through their blood cells to their brain and so they can survive the winter. While they don't eat during hibernation, they do need water. They take this in through special patches on their stomachs and upper legs.

SPRING AND MATING

Frogs come out of hibernation in spring when the water temperature rises. Mating and egg-laying take place in the pond where the frogs were born. The males are already hibernating there. The females usually hibernate in damp places nearby. When the females arrive at the pond, mating happens. Male frogs have special nuptial pads on their hands and they hold on to the female. The eggs are laid into the water and soon swell up to form frogspawn.

The adults leave the pond shortly after this. The eggs hatch out into tadpoles, which have to look after themselves and find their own food. They grow up to become adult frogs.

Nuptial pad

Tadpoles

Frogspawn

Tadpole

RISING FROM THE DEAD

Imagine the scene. There is a thing living in the soil in the garden underneath the grass. It slithers around, feeding on bacteria and fungal cells, getting bigger and bigger. Then one night in autumn after heavy rainfall, it bursts up and covers a patch of grass with what looks like dog's vomit. For that is its name – the Dog's vomit slime mould.

GROWING MOULD

The Dog's vomit slime mould continues to move slowly, about 10 centimetres per day, covering new bits of grass. It can even climb a tree to eat the fungi that grow there. Eventually, it hardens up and the insides produce millions of tiny spores that are blown away by the wind. Each spore can grow into another slime mould under the ground if it lands in the right place.

It wasn't me – I didn't do it!

Well, it wasn't there last night ...

Two stages of Dog's vomit slime mould

In early summer after wet weather and thunderstorms, thunderworms can appear overnight on plants in our gardens and polytunnels. These are long, very long — sometimes up to 50 centimetres long – and look like threadlike roundworms. They lay eggs on plants and then die when this job is done. The eggs are eaten by grasshoppers and caterpillars, and they hatch out inside these creatures. The young worms grow by digesting the body fluids of their host. When they are big enough to live on their own, the worms leave their host and enter the soil, where we never notice them until it rains heavily again in June and they emerge and climb up on our plants to lay eggs all over again.

White thunderworm. Thunderworms can be white or black, depending on the species.

SLIMY AND SLITHERY

Snails and slugs are molluscs. This means that they belong to a group of animals that have no legs. They are covered in slime and move by sliding on their undersides. They have four horns on their head and have eyes at the ends of the top two horns; they use the bottom two horns to smell. They have all their teeth on their tongue. Snails also have a shell attached to them that they can hide in, closing a door – called an operculum – after them.

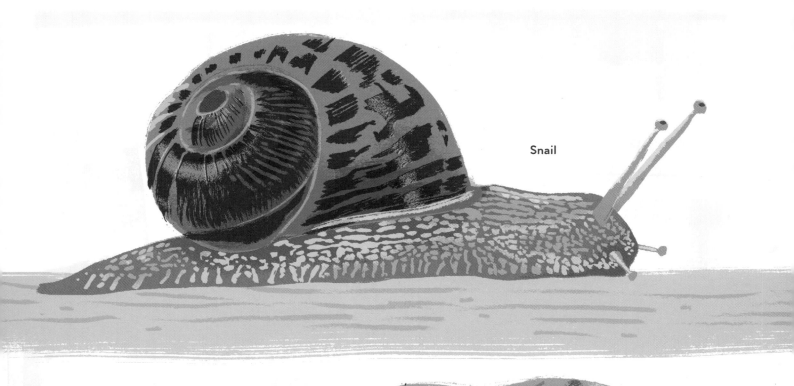

Snail

MALE AND FEMALE

Snails and slugs are both male and female at the same time. They can all lay eggs, but they need to mate first. They must find another snail or slug to mate with. They cannot mate with themselves.

Operculum – the closed door of a living snail

MATING

Great Grey slugs mate up in the air. First, two slugs climb up a tree and out on to an overhanging branch. Then they slowly twist the thick slime that covers their bodies into a strong, sticky rope, and they travel down this rope through the air. When they are about halfway down, they stop and come together, both in an upside-down position. Mating lasts for about an hour. Then one slug drops to the ground and the other one climbs back up on to the branch, eating the twisted, slimy rope as it goes. Both lay about a hundred eggs in the soil soon after this.

Large Black slug

Kerry slug

27

WAR CRIES AND LOVE SONGS

Birds singing together early on summer mornings is known as the dawn chorus. But it is only the males that do the singing. Female birds do not sing during the dawn chorus. Female robins have a territory of their own in winter and sing only in winter to defend it. No females of other Irish species do this.

MARKING TERRITORY

The males sing for two reasons only. The first reason is to claim their territory.
The robin singing loudly in the hedge is telling all the other male robins that this is his place and that he will defend it. The neighbouring robin sings back, and the boundary of their territories is set between them.

Male robin

ATTRACTING FEMALES

Birds also sing to attract a female. The female hears the song and comes to investigate. Female robins look exactly like male robins. The singing male thinks this is another male and goes to attack it, but the female doesn't fight back. Eventually the male realises that the other robin is a female. They go on to build a nest together and rear up to five young. The male continues to sing every morning at dawn to be sure that no other male will enter his territory and take the spiders and caterpillars that he wants for his chicks.

Female robin

THE BIRD WITH NO NEST

The cuckoo is a native Irish bird. It is born in Ireland, although it spends most of the year in Africa. Male cuckoos arrive from Africa in April and can be heard calling 'cuck-oo' as they fly around suitable breeding territory. Female cuckoos do not make this call.

MATING AND EGG-LAYING

Mating takes place in the early mornings, and, unlike other birds, females lay their eggs in the afternoons.

Cuckoos do not build a nest. In Ireland, the female lays an egg in the nest of another bird – the Meadow pipit (in Irish, *Giolla na Cuaiche* – the cuckoo's servant) – which is much smaller. She finds the pipits' nest on the ground when the parent bird is absent. Quickly, the cuckoo takes out one egg with her bill and lays her own egg, which looks very like the pipits' egg, there instead. She does this at least ten times in ten different meadow pipits' nests, which she can easily find as she was reared in such a nest herself.

Adult cuckoo

Young cuckoo

THE CUCKOO IN THE NEST

When the meadow pipit returns, she doesn't notice anything. Twelve days later, the cuckoo's egg hatches out first. The baby cuckoo throws out all the other eggs and so it is the only chick that the meadow pipits have to rear. This is just as well as the baby cuckoo grows to be many times bigger than the meadow pipits, who eventually have to stand on the cuckoo's back to feed it.

Meanwhile, once all the eggs are laid, the parent cuckoos go back to Africa in July, leaving the young birds to be raised by the meadow pipits. Cuckoos never see or hear their birth parents. Yet, by the end of August, each one leaves the nest and flies all the way to Africa by itself – their brains just know the way.

Meadow pipit

A VERY SHORT CHILDHOOD

All birds start out life inside eggs laid by their mother.
Most of our garden birds lay more than one egg.

BLUE TITS

Blue tits often lay ten eggs in their nest – one egg every day. It takes at least ten days for all the eggs to be laid. Then the female sits on them, incubating them, until they hatch out, fourteen days later. The male brings in the food for her during this time. All the eggs hatch out on the same day, even though the first egg was laid ten days before the last one.

EARLY DAYS

When the Blue tits hatch out, they have no feathers. Both parents work hard to feed them with small caterpillars, greenflies and spiders. Every day, each parent makes 500 visits to feed the hungry chicks. The female stays with them at night to keep them warm, while the male sleeps in a nearby tree.

After eighteen days they are fully grown and have all their feathers. They are ready to fly. Usually, they all leave the nest very early on a June morning and fly to trees and bushes in the garden. They never come back to the nest again. They must find their own food now, although sometimes their parents will help for a few days. By the following April they are mature enough to find a mate and start breeding.

SQUIRRELS DON'T HIBERNATE

We have two species of squirrel in Ireland: the Red squirrel and the Grey squirrel. They can both climb trees, and they live in nests called dreys, which they build from sticks. They collect nuts in autumn and store these in hidden places so that they can eat them in winter when there is nothing else to eat. Squirrels do not hibernate. They sleep at night, and they wake up every morning to go and look for food.

GREY OR RED

Grey squirrels are bigger than Red squirrels. They are an American species that were brought to Castle Forbes in County Longford in 1911 by the British Duke of Buckingham. Six squirrels in a wicker basket were a wedding present. They were let go into the woods, and all our Grey squirrels today are descended from them.

Grey squirrel

NATIVE RED SQUIRREL

The Red squirrel is smaller than the Grey and can run out to the thinnest branches to escape from its deadly enemy – the Pine marten. The Grey, which feeds on the ground, is more easily caught by the Pine marten, and indeed by dogs let off their leashes when out for a walk.

Red squirrel

FEEDING

In spring and summer, when the nuts are all gone, squirrels will eat shoots, buds and the bark of trees. Grey squirrels, which are much bolder, will even raid our gardens and help themselves to strawberries.

BATS AND THEIR SUPERPOWERS

Bats are the only mammals that can fly. The nine species of bats in Ireland all hunt at night for food. Most bats catch insects in the air. Some can pick them up with their feet, off leaves or off the ground.

DAUBENTON'S BAT

Daubenton's bat hunts over water, catching flies in the air or scooping up insects from the water with its tail. How can they do all this when it is pitch dark? Despite what some people think, bats are not blind, but to be able to fly in complete darkness they have a special ability – a superpower, as it were.

ECHO-LOCATION

Bats can echo-locate. This means that they can locate, or find, their prey by listening to the echoes of sound waves that they send out. Each bat species makes a particular sound. We can't hear these high-pitched sounds. When this sound bounces off an object, it is echoed back to the bat, and so the bat knows where the insect it is chasing is. Its ears act like satellite dishes and pick up the sounds. Bats won't fly into your hair, unless your head is covered in moths or mosquitoes!

HIBERNATING

Irish bats only eat insects and invertebrates. In winter, when it is too cold for this food source, the bats sleep. They hibernate from October to April in a special place – somewhere where they won't freeze. During the summer they might live in a house attic or in a special bat box, but in winter they need a different roost. This could be in an underground cave, a graveyard crypt or in the cellar of an old house.

A DIRTY JOB

Flies are very important to the environment. They help to break down and recycle the corpses of dead creatures. In turn, they are food for birds that catch them in flight, or for spiders that trap them in their webs.

Bluebottles

NOISE AND TASTE BUDS

Bluebottles are large metallic blue flies that come into our houses, looking for food.

They make a very annoying noise when flying. This sound is a hum made by the very fast movements of their wings, which beat 200 times per second as they fly. When they land, the sound stops.

These flies have taste buds on their legs, so they walk on things to see if they taste nice enough for them to eat. They love meat, which can be dead animals or birds, dog droppings or our hamburgers. Their feet can be covered in nasty germs, which they can put on our food as they walk on it.

FEEDING

Bluebottles have a particular way of eating food. First, they vomit up a strong liquid on to it. This dissolves the meat and forms a little puddle. Then they suck up all the liquid through their tongue, which is long and is shaped like a hollow straw.

If there is a lot of food, such as a dead bird or mouse, the females will lay eggs on it. The young hatch out into white maggots and start feeding and growing, quickly using up all the food. Then they become a pupa and soon afterwards emerge as adult bluebottles.

Bluebottle maggots

39

THE FLOWER PRISON

Most flowers produce a lovely smell to attract insects, but not the Arum lily. This woodland plant makes a horrible scent. Why does it do this?

STINK TRAP

The Arum lily smell is made by the purple stalk, sticking up in the middle of the flower – the spadix. This stinky smell attracts flies, making them think that there is a tasty meal of rotten meat inside the flower. The flies become trapped as the gap in the side of the spadix has stiff hairs that bend down to allow them in but won't bend up to allow them out.

POLLINATION

Eventually, one or two flies arrive that have escaped from another lily. These flies are covered with lily pollen that gets rubbed against the female part of the flower and so pollinates it. Then the stiff guard hairs collapse, letting the trapped flies out. They too get covered with pollen as they leave. They often visit another Arum lily, pollinating it and letting the trapped flies there escape.

DINNER WITH DIFFICULTY

Imagine being a bird that eats fish, but that cannot swim. This is the case for the kingfisher and the grey heron.

KINGFISHER

The kingfisher eats freshwater fish and is to be found by rivers. How does it fish if it cannot swim? It perches on overhanging tree branches, above the river, and watches the water. When a fish swims by, the kingfisher leaps off into the river, grabs the fish in its beak and flies back to its branch, before it drowns. Then, it swallows the fish in one gulp.

GREY HERON

The Grey heron is a large bird, but it too cannot swim. With its long legs, it stands in water that is deep enough for fish and waits for fish to pass by. The heron then moves very quickly to catch the fish in its beak and swallow it, headfirst. If it swallowed it tail first, the scales of the fish would be rubbed up the wrong way and the heron might choke.

ANIMALS WE LOVE TO HATE

There are animals that some people don't like because of what they might do to us or our livestock. I wonder what the animals might say if they were asked if they liked us. Humans interfere with and often destroy the habitats of these creatures, forcing them to come looking for food closer to our homes.

FOXES

Many people do not like foxes because they sneak into their hen houses and kill all their hens. The hens cannot fly away and the fox keeps killing until all is quiet. In the wild when a fox attacks a roosting group of birds, most of them can fly away and escape, and the fox only gets one or two. It is their nature not to stop killing until all prey is dead or gone. Foxes also kill rats and mice, which otherwise might eat our food and give us diseases, so they can be important allies to us.

BADGERS

Some people think that a badger will come out of its underground sett and bite their leg as they walk through the field. Such a thing could never happen as badgers have a great sense of smell and keep well away from humans. They eat lots of soil grubs, such as those of the cockchafer, which otherwise would damage the farmers' grain and grass crops.

MAGPIES

Most people dislike magpies. These noisy birds build nests in tall trees in urban areas. They kill the young of smaller birds and feed them to their own chicks. But they do not collect shiny objects and put them in their nests.

GULLS

Most of us don't like the seagulls that fly around our cities and towns, screeching, building nests on our roofs and eating our food — sometimes even swiping ice-cream or chips out of our hands. These birds are Herring gulls and Black-backed gulls. Their natural habitat is on grassy clifftops by the sea, where they feed on fish and crabs. But we have taken more than our fair share of the fish and built houses and golf clubs on their nesting sites, so the gulls are forced to come to our urban areas, where they feed on the food waste that we leave lying around. These clever birds can even rip open plastic rubbish bags to find food.

THEY FEED ON HUMAN BLOOD

Head lice need humans to live on. These wingless insects jump on to our hair from someone else who has them and whose head is close to ours.

ADULTS

Adult lice are about the size of a grain of rice. They have six legs with a strong claw at the end of each and they hold on very tightly to a strand of hair with these. Washing your hair will not get rid of them.

Head louse

HUMAN BLOOD

The only food a head louse eats is human blood. Their biting parts are usually hidden away in their head. When they are hungry, they stick out three sharp needles and pierce our skin. Then they pump our blood up into their head and down into their intestines. Their poo is dried drops of blood that go into our hair.

LAYING EGGS

A female can live on our hair for a month and during that time she lays up to ten eggs (nits) every day. She sticks these on to other hairs very near to the scalp. Seven days later, the young hatch out and start feeding on our blood too. It doesn't feel painful, but it is terribly itchy.

The best way to get rid of lice is to comb the hair with a special comb that makes them let go of the hair. You need to do this every day for a week to make sure that even the newly hatched ones are all gone. You can even get electric zapping combs that make a noise when one is caught. The eggs are very difficult to remove. There are always some left! This is why you have to wait till the lice hatch out and keep combing for a week. Chemical treatments are not good as head lice can become immune to these.

Nits on human scalp

FLEAS AND BED BUGS

Human fleas and bed bugs feed on our blood too, although they don't live on us all the time. The fleas leap on to us when they are hungry. Bed bugs bite when we are asleep. Both fleas and bed bugs are much rarer than head lice.

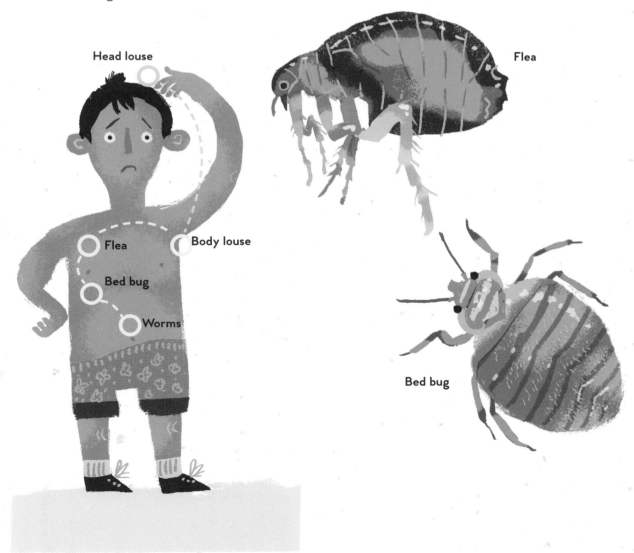

Head louse

Flea

Body louse

Flea

Bed bug

Worms

Bed bug

GLOWING UNDERWATER

There are creatures in the sea around our coasts that glow in the dark.

NOCTILUCA

Noctiluca are tiny, one-celled animals that live in colonies on the surface of the sea. They make the surface of the sea sparkle at night, and much more light is produced if the water is disturbed by waves or by a boat. The light is produced by a molecule in the animal's body called luciferin, a molecule that, when it reacts with oxygen, produces light. This is a cold light called bioluminescence.

ANGLERFISH

Anglerfish that swim around in the sea can do this too. These are large fish with huge teeth. They have what looks like a nice piece of bait dangling in front of their mouth, and it is this bait that can glow in the dark. When a small fish comes along to eat the bait, the anglerfish gobbles it instead.

GLOWING JELLYFISH

There are even glowing jellyfish in our waters too. One of these is called the Crystal jellyfish. When disturbed, it gives off a green-blue glow because it has more than a hundred light-producing cells surrounding its umbrella-like bell. So, it can glow in the dark as it swims along.

MANCATCHERS – Amphibians or Reptiles?

Mancatcher is an old name given to newts because people were afraid that if they fell asleep outdoors with their mouth open, one would go into their mouth and right down into their stomach. Then they would get a terrible hunger that could never be satisfied, no matter how much they ate.

SMOOTH NEWT

Ireland's Smooth newt does nothing of the sort. It is an amphibian with four legs and a long tail. The male has a wavy crest and very bright colours during the spring mating season. The newts only visit ponds in spring, and the female lays a long string of individual eggs there. While both male and female newts are in the water, they eat any frogs' eggs or tadpoles that they find. So, there are never frogs and newts in the same pond — not for long anyway.

The female newt is above the male (with crest) here. Newts are 10 centimetres long in total, with the tail making up half its length.

Common lizard, also called Viviparous lizard. Fully grown, it is 15 centimetres in length.

LIZARDS

Lizards have the same shape as newts, but as they are reptiles, they have a scaly skin and never go into water. They are much bigger too, with an extremely long tail. They can break off their tail and grow another if a predator such as a stoat grabs it. The female of our Irish species – the Viviparous lizard – does not lay eggs. She gives birth to tiny baby lizards during the summer months. That is what 'viviparous' means.

The easiest way to tell the difference between a newt and a lizard is to look at the front legs. Newts have four toes on each front foot and lizards have five.

Lizard with broken tail

GOING SIDEWAYS

Moving in a forward direction makes sense most of the time, especially when hunting for food or avoiding enemies. You can see where you are going and what is in front of you.

ANIMALS OF THE SEA

However, in the sea, some animals move in other directions. Crabs can only walk sideways. This is because the knee joints on their legs – the second joints – only move sideways, so they find it impossible to walk frontways.
   How can they see where they are going? Their eyes are on stalks and they can swivel them in the direction they are going.

Velvet
swimming
crab

SWIMMING

Some crabs, like the Velvet swimming crab, can also swim, using the last pair of their ten legs as paddles. They usually swim sideways, but they can swim backwards as well.

Lobsters can also swim backwards by flexing and unflexing their tail underneath them. They do this to escape from enemies and they can move very fast, reaching speeds of 18 kilometres per hour. However, they do walk forwards.

Lobster

DEFENDED BY PRICKLES

Hedgehogs are thought to have been brought to Ireland over a thousand years ago by the Vikings as a food source. They roasted and ate them.

CARNIVORES

Hedgehogs are carnivores that come out at night to look for food. They eat slugs, beetles, caterpillars, snails and earthworms. In winter when none of this food is available, they hibernate to survive. They slow down their metabolism and live off their body fat. Their heart rate drops from 190 to 20 beats per minute. Their body temperature can go as low as 4 degrees Celsius from a summer high of 34 degrees. Hedgehogs are all in hibernation by the end of October and will wake up again in April, when the weather warms up again.

They roll into a ball to defend themselves from being eaten. Only the badger is able to uncurl them to eat them.

PLANTS THAT EAT ANIMALS

In Ireland there are several plants that eat animals. They do this because they grow in bogs where the soil is poor and lacks nutrients. The plants get these missing nutrients from the insects they catch.

SUNDEW

The Sundew has round leaves that are covered with hairs. At the end of each hair is a drop of very sticky glue. When a fly lands on a leaf, it gets stuck and cannot fly away. Then the plant slowly dissolves the body of the fly and digests all its soft bits. Only the hard outer parts of the fly are left.

PITCHER PLANT

The Pitcher plant is an American species that was first planted on some Irish bogs in 1906. Its leaves are shaped like little jugs. These jugs have sweet nectar at the top and are half full of rainwater. When an insect lands to drink the nectar, it slips on the waxy, slippery leaf, falls into the well below and is trapped. The plant quickly devours it.

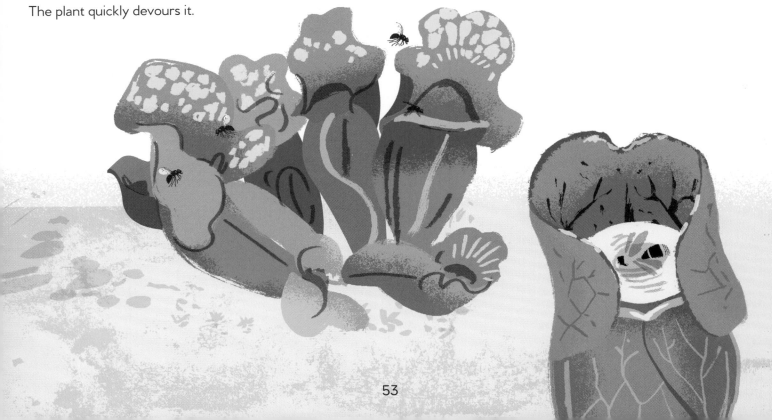

DO CUCKOOS SPIT?

In June we often see plants such as lavender or nettles covered in what looks like white spit. Long ago, some people called this 'cuckoo spit', as they thought that the cuckoo spat on plants as he cleared his throat to call 'cuck-oo'.

THE TRUE STORY

The white 'cuckoo spit' is just a blob of white suds containing a small, green wingless insect with dark brown eyes. This is the young of a brown insect called a froghopper that lives on the leaves of trees. Female froghoppers lay their eggs in slits in the lavender or nettle plants and then die.

FROGHOPPER TRICK

In May the froghopper eggs hatch out into little green insects – the nymph stage. These feed on the juice and sap in the plant, and they suck up so much that lots of it goes right through them and out their bottom end. Air gets mixed with this liquid as it passes through their bodies, and so lots of suds are formed, covering each insect.

This allows the insect to continue feeding in peace as its enemies – the birds – are fooled and they never realise that a tasty meal is hiding inside what looks just like spit.

The young froghopper spends a whole month like this, growing, until finally it changes into a brown adult froghopper and hops away into the trees around.

Cuckoo spit

Froghopper nymph

Froghopper

Froghopper

Cuckoo spit

WASHED UP FROM THE DEPTHS

After a storm, it is possible to find animals that usually live under the sea washed up on the seashore.

MERMAID'S PURSES

Mermaid's purses are empty squares of hard seaweed-like material with strings at the corners. What was once in these purses was not money but the young of fish such as rays, skates or dogfish.

The females of these fish lay these containers of young fish, which they have made inside themselves, and they tie them by the corner strings to seaweed at the bottom of the sea. The small fish quickly grow big enough to leave the pouch and catch their own food. Then, when a storm comes, the empty purses are torn from the seaweed and washed up on the shore.

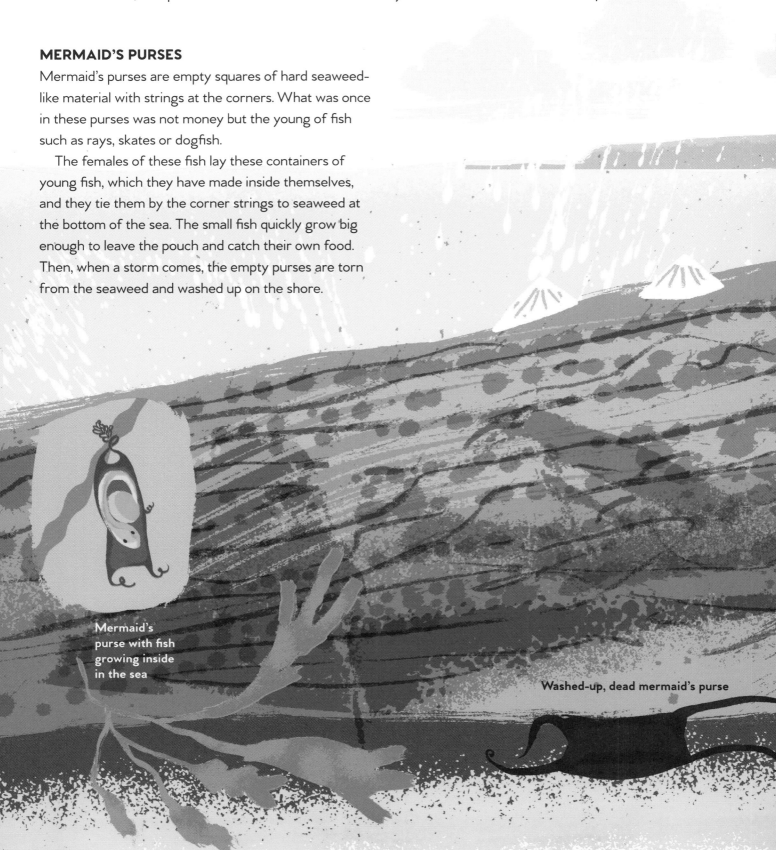

Mermaid's purse with fish growing inside in the sea

Washed-up, dead mermaid's purse

DEAD MAN'S FINGERS

Timber from wrecks can be washed up too. Sometimes these planks are covered in Dead man's fingers. These are soft corals that grow deep down in the sea and feed on small particles in the water, which they catch by waving themselves around. People seeing these corals underwater thought that they were the size and shape of human fingers.

Goose barnacles

Dead man's fingers

GOOSE BARNACLES

Wood that washes up on the shore can also be covered in long black and white shellfish called Goose barnacles. These live on shipwrecks and feed on particles in the ocean. Long ago, people thought that they were not fish at all but young geese – Barnacle geese. These geese come to Ireland in winter to feed on our snow-free grass; they never breed here. When people saw the geese migrate over the sea and come back with young geese, they imagined that somehow barnacles grew into geese. The truth is that these geese breed much further north than Ireland, in Greenland.

SLOWCOACHES

Fifteen thousand years ago, there was no wildlife in Ireland. It was nearing the end of the last ice age, and the country was covered in ice, as was much of Britain and northern Europe. All the wildlife was further south, where there was no ice. As the world became warmer, the ice melted. At this time, Ireland was joined to Britain, which was in turn joined to France. As the land was uncovered, the plants and animals spread north.

ISLANDS

More ice continued to melt as the world continued to warm up and the sea levels rose. After a thousand years, Ireland had become an island surrounded by water. Britain stayed joined to France for another thousand years before it too became an island. The slower-moving animals that had just made it into Britain, before the English channel separating it from France was formed, couldn't keep going to Ireland because of the Irish Sea.

Wild Irish goat

EUROPEAN ANIMALS THAT ARE NOT IN IRELAND

Moles that live under the soil in Britain never got here. Snakes were moving too slowly as well, and although three sorts of snakes (Adder, Grass snake and Smooth snake) got to Britain, they were there too late to get across the Irish Sea to Ireland.

Genets, Beech or Stone martens and Chamois are all examples of animals that are to be found in France but not in Britain or Ireland.

Red deer

Smooth snake

Grass snake

Mole

Badger

Adder

Beech marten

Genet

Chamois

59

Éanna Ní Lamhna is one of the best-known public figures in Ireland, in particular as a biologist, environmental and wildlife consultant, radio and television presenter, author and educator. Éanna has one of the most instantly recognisable voices on Irish radio and has been for many years a member of the panel of experts on RTÉ's wildlife programme *Mooney Goes Wild*. She also served for five years as president of the national environmental charity An Taisce, and is a former president of the Tree Council of Ireland. Originally from Louth, she now lives in Dublin. Éanna is the author of several popular wildlife books, including *Talking Wild*, *Straight Talking Wild*, *Wild Things at School* and *Wild Dublin: Exploring Nature in the City*, shortlisted for the Reading Association of Ireland Award. Her most recent books, *Our Wild World: From the Birds and Bees to Our Boglands and the Ice Caps* and *Wild and Wonderful: Around the World with Éanna* were published in 2021 and 2022 by The O'Brien Press.

Brian Fitzgerald feels most at home illustrating children's picture books, encouraged by winning the International Silent Book Competition in Bologna. His most recent books are *You Can Do It, Rosie*, with author Elena Browne, *I Don't Want To Go To School*, *Does an Astronaut Drive a Tractor?* and *Does a Firefighter Fly a Rocket?* He has had the pleasure of seeing five of his books brought to life on 'Vooks'. He lives and works in Dún Laoghaire.

First published 2023 by
The O'Brien Press Ltd, 12 Terenure Road East, Rathgar, Dublin 6, D06 HD27, Ireland.
Tel: +353 1 4923333; Fax: +353 1 4922777; E-mail: books@obrien.ie; Website: obrien.ie
The O'Brien Press is a member of Publishing Ireland.

ISBN: 978-1-78849-408-3

8 7 6 5 4 3 2 1
26 25 24 23

Printed and bound by Drukarnia Skleniarz, Poland.
The paper in this book is produced using pulp from managed forests

To my grandchildren Alice, Teddy and Charles.
Éanna Ní Lamhna

Published in

DUBLIN
UNESCO
City of Literature

Growing up with
O'BRIEN
obrien.ie